The Fashion Annual

THE ALGORITHM EDITION
2018/19

Lynne Coleman

Luath Press Limited

EDINBURGH

www.luath.co.uk

First published 2018

ISBN: 978-1-912147-71-7

The paper used in this book is recyclable. It is made from low chlorine pulps produced in a low energy, low emissions manner from renewable forests.

Printed and bound by
Bell & Bain Ltd., Glasgow

Typeset in 13 point Bodoni by 3btype.com

All contributed photographs reproduced with the kind permission of each contributor.

The author's right to be identified as author of this work under the Copyright, Designs and Patents Act 1988 has been asserted.

© Lynne Coleman 2018

To the fearless women around the world

who support each other.

You are awesome.

And to my very own fearless woman,

Big Red,

our journey in 2014

paved the way for this book.

I love you.

Acknowledgements

THE CREATIVE TEAM
To you crazy bunch of creatives who took the time to come on this journey with me, thank you for your time and talent. I am honoured to work with you and call you friends. I am so proud of what we achieved.

THE PUBLISHING TEAM
Getting a vision from thought to paper is a long process. Without your input and anchoring, this idea would have been rudderless and shipwrecked. Thank you for all your hard work Alice, Lauren, Maia and Gavin for believing in the concept. To Senga, we have walked this path for almost a decade together – there is no one I trust more with design than you, you've done a beautiful job. Thank you.

THE COMMUNICATIONS TEAM
Mel, you are the best in the business. But above all of that you are a fabulous friend. The stories we share could keep gossip columnists in business for years... ha! Thank you for introducing me to the fearless and fabulous Federica – Fed, you understood this from the get-go, I'm so grateful to you.

MY MEN
To my trio of true love. Jamie, Gabriel and Rafe, thank you for giving me the best job in the world as your wife and mother. Big guy, there is no one I'd rather build this beautiful family with than you. No-one I'd rather belly-laugh with at the end of a day and no-one I'd rather run off to a date night with. Thank you for pushing me, challenging me and loving me. Your overachieving ways are utterly seductive and make me only marginally competitive...

Contents

The Age of Algorithm   6–11
Fear   12–29
Theatre of Lies   30–39
The Emancipation of Motherhood   40–57
Tits & Toes   58–73
Mathematics of the Face   74–89

Plastic   78–99
We've All Got To Eat   62–77
In Conversation with Osman   44–61
Colour Cult   18–43
Ode to Zelda   4–17
Contributors   2–3

Contents

The Age of Algorithm

Algorithm

1. a set of mathematical instructions or rules that will help to calculate an answer to a problem

2. a set of code used by social media platforms to analyse and predict which posts their customers want to see – therefore meaning content is no longer seen in order of publish date but, instead, in terms of relevancy

Images by Nuala Swan
Make-up Director: Jen Beattie for Blow Bridal
Shoot Concept by Fal Carberry for Blow Bridal
Hair: Jacqui Malcolm at Blow Colour Bar
Model: Lynne Coleman

This year has been rather noisy, right?

It's been hard to cut through the crap and see things clearly. Everyone appears divided on an array of issues that no-one is an expert on – from the cabbie getting me around the city to politicians around the world. In an age of algorithm-controlled information, opinion has trumped fact.

I have spent this year on maternity leave, watching the months unfold from the sidelines, like a movie-goer watching a salacious film, shrouded in darkness on the back row. Each day, as I scrolled through my phone, a surreal sense of denial would sweep over me. I struggled to believe that we were, and are, living in a world so divided by anger, hate, fear and stupidity. The online algorithms brought up both horrifying headlines and vacuous products. Real murder contrasted with smiley faced online-assassins paid to hawk on social media. Oh, and do you want a side of 'inspirational quote' with that?

I am a visual vulture. I'd spend my time flitting between breast feeding and scrolling through imagery pretending I didn't miss making it. You see, my life before babies was about creating pictures for newspapers and brands. Curating images for storytelling is boundlessly rewarding. Once that shot is taken, it can say more than a million words. That's the bit I bloody love.

The Fashion Annual uses a set of snaps to tell the stories of 2018/19, using fashion and photography as the pen and paper. Over the years I have been fortunate enough to accumulate the most incredible bunch of creative friends. Together, we set about storytelling the topics that have resonated with us over the last twelve months.

From our bare-faced inability to ban single use plastics in 'Plastic: We're Programmed Not To See It', to 'The Colour Cult', where we discuss how mental health issues perpetually plague people who, from the outside, look like they are having all the fun, it struck me that social media is to us what the tobacco industry was to people in the 1960s

I wanted to create a set of snaps that told the stories of 2018/19 using fashion and photography as the pen and paper.

as they tried to cover-up its dangers to ensure its survival – this stuff needs to come with a serious health warning. And so, I wanted the images to do the talking.

As we planned the book, the word algorithm kept arising – from election fraud on a global scale to small businesses scared to watch fictitious followers fluctuate each time an iOS update was released.

People's reactions to being stripped of a couple of thousand followers was like watching brokers balking as the stock market plummeted on Wall Street.

How can it be that important, we ask? Well, if your livelihood, political freedom and financial security relied upon having followers, wouldn't you be worried? It is important and yet, it seems, we care not a jot.

Someone said to me once that having a large social media following was akin to being rich in monopoly money. It's not real. It's a game.

But this is our lives – and we are all currently baws-deep copulating with code.

Because of that I took the word algorithm and spun it out – using it as the framework of the book.

In 'Theatre of Lies' I wanted to showcase the sinister side of growing up in an age where the hand-held device in your pocket is so powerful it can answer any question instantly – and, although this incredible piece of machinery has the ability to enlighten, with no teacher present to instil the importance of fact-checking, it can rapidly become a very dangerous tool for propaganda.

In 'The Mathematics of the Face', I wanted to show age, gender and race diversity to counterbalance a world of Photoshop, face tuning and fillers.

Through 'We've All Got to Eat' the tales of extreme poverty and excessive wealth came tumbling out of Manhattan.

'In Conversation with Osman' about the ferocious cycles of fashion and the speed at which it hurtles became bitter-sweet after hearing the sad news of Kate Spade taking her own life.

'Fear' was primarily about the feelings evoked by the word algorithm – we played around with the most commonly documented phobias and set about cementing them. What came back from that day transcended our theme, trivialising these common phobias, as Howey's powerful presence in front of the lens spoke volumes for the injustices happening to black men around the world. I remember thinking how much of a privilege being frightened of a spider in the safety of your own home would be in comparison to the fear felt by men being shackled into slavery or shot by police just because of their hue. Fearing for your freedom and your life in 2018/19 – that's the stuff of nightmares.

Midway through shooting the project, it was time for me to get brutally personal. Spellbound by Christina Ricci's portrayal of Zelda Fitzgerald I devoured her first season of *Z: The Beginning of Everything* like a full-cheeked hamster stockpiling nuts. Her story was always one that resonated with me; she and Margaret Macdonald Mackintosh have been huge sources of inspiration and fascination. The patriarchy and #metoo came flooding in as I revisited these sensational women who stood beside iconic husbands and yet were arguably more talented than either of them.

This paved the way for 'The Emancipation of Motherhood', exploring the impact that childbirth has on us as a gender, and the self imposed slavery we go through while caring, nurturing, feeding and clearing up after people who don't pay us, who never give us breaks or holidays and expect us to be there twenty-four hours a day. Although this is something we exhaustingly do with love, the empathy from society is comparable to 'couldn't give a fuck you brain-dead moron'. Cheers guys, kiss your mumma with that mouth?

I hope you enjoy the aesthetic we created. I pray it provokes thought. But, most importantly, I can't wait to look back on this annual in a decade and see the positive changes that came out of a year that felt so upside down.

Lynne

Lynne Coleman has worked with brands such as Burberry, Chanel, Mulberry, Liberty of London and Harvey Nichols, as well as championing young design talent in her career as a fashion writer and style columnist at the *Edinburgh Evening News*, and in-house stylist for *Scotland on Sunday*. You can frequently find her at the BBC, be it BBC Breakfast, Five Live, Radio 4 or Radio Scotland as their go-to fashion girl. She is the brand guardian of the world's only hand-crafted tartan mill, DC Dalgliesh and has her own knitwear line called Cross Cashmere.

When asked what algorithm meant to her, Ellie Morag said

Fear

Enlisting the help of muse Howey Ejegi, the pair depict phobias that resonate with both of them.

Images by Ellie Morag

Model: Howey Ejegi

Acrophobia

fear of heights

Aviophobia

```
F
E   O
A   FLYING
R
```

Aphenphosm phobia

fear of intimacy

Atychiphobia

fear of failure

Claustrophobia

fear of
small
spaces

Mysophobia

fear of germs

Thanatophobia

fear of death

Theatre of Lies

How do you navigate
a world of code
when you're
already a native?

Images by Brian Sweeney
Concept by Lynne Coleman

Models:
Adam Holmes
Zazou Wycherley

An unremarkable conversation one soggy Saturday with my then six-year-old led to some quite serious thinking about the illusion of theatre.

He had been sucked into YouTube for twenty minutes or so before he began telling me that the kids on screen had snuck into a shop at 3am to see if it was haunted – the backbone of this chat being could HE stay up until 3am to see if things were haunted. Without missing a beat I informed him the clip wasn't real.

He begged to differ.

You see the kids in the clip weren't TV stars. They were just kids with a YouTube account uploading whatever they liked to the big bad web. There was no disclosure to say if this was reality, fiction, factual or even a documentary. My training as a journalist always has me

questioning sources, even subconsciously, but trying to articulate why I didn't believe the three kids in the clip to my six-year-old was a lot more complicated than I had imagined.

To him, it was real. It was on a screen, it must be true.

Dismissing the discussion once we had established the ins and outs of fact and fiction, we all went about the rest of our day unscathed. But a seed had been planted and I was now on high alert over the hijacking of young minds.

It never occurred to me that this could be happening to grown men and women all over the globe on a daily basis. As everyone ignores each other in their offline world to talk to people in their online world it appears that opinions hold more weight than fact, and fact-checking is as redundant as dial-up internet.

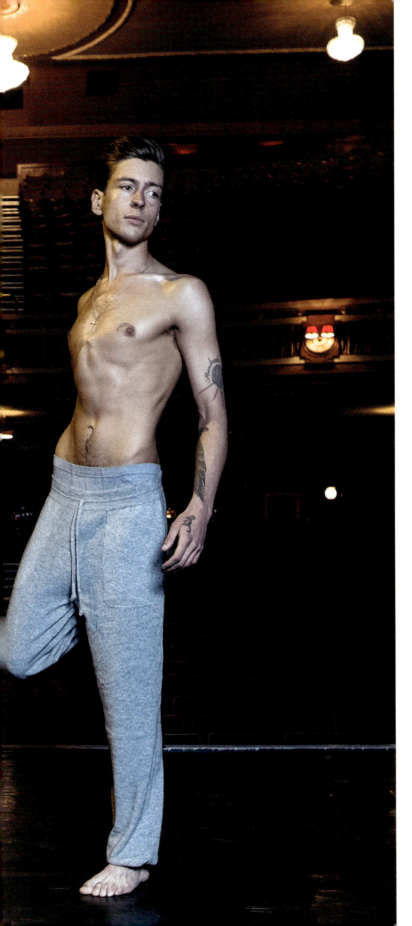

Looking at the malleable minds of our kids, it is terrifying to think we are polluting not only their planet but their thoughts and freedom too.

For this shoot I wanted the stage which Zazou and Adam stood on to be a metaphor for their online life. What you see on stage is an illusion. A show. Curation. Where actors are fed lines by someone else's hand.

I hope one day we will all see the internet with artistic licence, but for now it just seems too dangerous a place to play.

The Emancipation of Motherhood

In conversation with Katie Danger

Images by Christina Kernohan

Model: Katie Danger

Styled by Katie Danger and Lynne Coleman

Make-up: Molly Jane Sheridan

With thanks to Glasgow University

Before you become a mum,
mums are invisible to you.

The day we shot this pictorial the very pregnant Katie and I headed west with our toddlers to the majestic cloisters at Glasgow University. This was a special shoot for us. A few weeks earlier, Ireland had just repealed the 8th amendment and it felt good supporting each other, with our kids, to go and create imagery that really meant something to us both. Joining us was our photographer and, also pregnant, pal, Christina Kernohan, and Molly, who was on make-up. The day ran smoothly as our boys played around the ancient courtyards of one of the world's oldest educational institutions. Midway through, Katie had a pregnancy dizzy spell, so we took it easy, finished up and knew that there'd be a seat waiting for us on the train for the fifty-minute journey back to Edinburgh.

What transpired on that journey was the emancipation of motherhood in a microcosm. Travelling off-peak, we popped our buggies in the designated seating area where the chairs flip up. We then grabbed a table with our toddlers. Halfway through the journey, a lovely couple of octogenarians got on. The older lady had a fold down wheelchair but she walked on and sat in a seat as her chair went in the final seat that folded away. It was then that Katie and I were intimidated and made to feel worthless by two female staff members who were bothered by our buggies. They told us off like naughty schoolgirls for using their company's designated area *correctly*. The whole carriage got to hear the earful, some looked on sympathetically others rolled their eyes. I mean, really, we're just such an inconvenience us mothers... ffs!

Katie: I was thinking the other day, when I was on a shoot, that mums are invisible if you are not a mum. Some of the team were moaning about one girl they work with because she was a new mum and running late. The people moaning were girls, so I said: 'You wait ten years until you have babies, then you'll see what it's like to be a mum and work'. You could see their judgment in their eyes – and I thought to myself YOU JUST DON'T UNDERSTAND!

Lynne: No, motherhood doesn't evoke empathy. You know that day on the train I really felt like we were third class citizens – like we didn't even matter. I suppose that's the hard thing: society views and treats you one way as a woman and in a very different way as a mother.

Katie: I know, people take you more seriously as a woman. I think that since I've had Sonny I don't get taken as seriously for jobs – I don't get asked to do as many. Don't get me wrong, I bet that a lot of it is to do with the fact that I can't always do it but people just stop asking. Then you see other people that you have worked with in the past get jobs that you used to do – it's a bit aaaaaaaaaaahhh!

Lynne: The odd thing about that, too, is your tolerance to work stuff changes – there are things now that I just wouldn't do.

Katie: Absolutely.

Lynne: You change as a person yet everything else around you doesn't change, so you become isolated. We live in a world now where we don't support each other, as women, as much as we used to. Think back to those 1950s housewives…

Katie: Who would look after your child if you had to go and do something nowadays?

Lynne: Absolutely! And, you know, I am fearful when I leave my child – even with a relative.

Katie: Completely. If I leave Sonny with his grandma I still say just remember how fast he is or take his hand when crossing the road. You do freak out. Which is silly.

Lynne: Yeah, because we don't usually leave them.

Katie: Totally. Once I have had this baby and go back to work properly in April, childcare is going to cost around £130 a day.

Lynne: Who's making enough money that they can find £130 a day on top of the money they have been making previously just so they can live life?? It's just not sustainable. It's like financially imprisoning yourself.

Katie: Yep.

Lynne: But I suppose it means that women get really creative, we have to work out how to make it work for ourselves.

Katie: Yeah, and I think even with our partners being one hundred per cent there for us, supporting us to raise the children and continue our careers, as women you still feel like, as the mum, you are the primary parent whilst still wanting to be a provider. In your head you are conflicted because there just isn't enough time to satisfy it all. I want to be a full-time member of the working world and I also want to be a full-time mum. Actually the term 'full-time mum' annoys me – just because I'm at work doesn't mean I'm mothering part-time. It's still full-on all the time.

Lynne: The juggle is hard. We underestimate ourselves in the multitasking.

Katie: You also definitely lose your identity a bit as a mother. You aren't as young and fun as you used to be. And when you do go out and have a few drinks you are steaming – it's so embarrassing! Ha!

Lynne: Ha! But there is a creative shift. I remember certainly feeling, when Gabriel (my oldest child) was first born, that I needed to work smarter. And this has led to where I am at today, and it's the same with you, our careers have been sculpted by the personal choices we have made. Other women aren't as fortunate and haven't had that luxury – because that's what it is, a luxury.

Katie: We are so lucky we can actually mould our careers, do what we want to do and be supported.

Lynne: When I first started out, there was not that much money and I was trying to prove myself and build a work reputation. I was doing that when I had my first baby, it was really hard. I was in a one bedroom flat sleeping on a sofa bed. You just have to get on with it and keep moving forward.

Katie: I was reading something the other day about celebs which said there aren't just actors or just singers anymore – everyone's roles are hyphenated. You know: actor-entrepreneur-activist. I think as you get older you are not as interested in the solo subject that you studied when you were seventeen, you do change and evolve. And actually, as a mum, we can adapt to different interests and pressures so much easier – for example, I started a music company with a friend to put on gigs for parents and kids. You know I love music and taking Sonny to cool things, so it seemed like a good fit. Also I love clothes and styling so I get to work in those areas too. You can change things, bring it all together. Being freelance really helps with that. However, the downside of it is the financial element – not getting maternity pay or even having a job to go back to once you've taken time off. After all, your clients have had to find new stylists – things have changed.

Lynne: Totally. The world moves on. As a person who took five years away from my career on maternity leave, I have five years less experience than someone who has continued to work and moved

with the world. This is the hard reality about the gender pay gap – the inequality happens because of the time women have to take to carry, give birth to and care for their children.

When you think about the logistical fairness of it all, taking men and women out of the equation and basing this on you and me, for example, we were at the exact same point in our careers when we were in our twenties. Then, when I stopped work to have my first child, you continued to work full-time so over that two year period you gained so much more experience. Then, when I came back to work, everything that I had learnt before was still relevant but not as up to date. As a freelancer you're probably charging more on a day rate and are better connected, whereas if someone has worked continuously for a decade that person has moved into a different pay bracket altogether. I think we are naive when we think about maternity leave because it's not a flexible thing in our society – we are fighting so many inequality battles. But in this current climate of political correctness, it almost feels like I'm being anti-feminist to say my gender dictates my choices – but it does. My biology dictates my choices.

Katie: But it does, Lynne. Look at the nine months you are pregnant for even before you have the child – you are so tired, so sick, can't concentrate. Your head is screwed and you are trying to really make a good impression at work because you want to return to work and you know everyone is watching you differently. And no matter if you only take a week off for maternity leave, you are still, during those nine months, not in a good place...

Lynne: Even if you are having the best text book pregnancy – you are still growing a human – that's distracting and all-consuming!

It *is* all-consuming.

Tits & Toes

In conversation with Jessica Bird

All illustrations by Jessica Bird

Jessica Bird, illustrator de jour, is the talk of London Town.

Lynne: When did you first move to London?

Jess: December 2014. I first came down for a three week internship with Roksanda. Then I did a month design internship with Jonathan Saunders.

Lynne: It doesn't get cooler than those two, right?

Jess: Yeah, Roksanda is now my ultimate favourite brand, but I didn't know her before and I got the internship through my friend, Jen. She was flying out to Paris to help in the showroom, they needed an extra pair of hands and I was doing nothing and was on a severe come down in Aberdeen post uni, so I went. We did a week in the Paris showroom doing everything from dressing models, sewing little bits…

Lynne: So basically getting submerged in the running of a label?

Jess: Yeah, it was quite an eye-opener as I'd never done any internships while I'd been at uni so it was great to experience what the fashion world was really like. And once the week was done I went back to Aberdeen to graduate from Gray's School of Art and then came back down to do three more weeks with Roksanda in London to help out with the fashion show.

Lynne: And that was the proper start to your career?

Jess: Yeah, from there I did a more design-based internship with Jonathan Saunders where I did spec drawing – technical drawings, mainly computer-based stuff. After that I came home for a bit, then returned to London for a paid internship with Hugo Boss, which came about through another friend. This lasted for six months. I worked as a wholesale assistant in head office – it was not what I wanted to do long-term but it opened my eyes to the business side of fashion, which was really great to see. While I was in London, I needed to do something creative as I knew I'd go crazy if I didn't, so my friend, Chris, put me in touch with Joshua Kane. I gave him a message asking if I could come in and help with sewing or anything just to get me creative again. So I'd work for Hugo Boss from 9–5, then I'd go to Josh's in the evening and help out with anything he needed. When my time came to an end at Hugo Boss, Josh had space to take me on full-time as a design assistant.

Lynne: That's so good, that's what happens when you put yourself out there. It was during this time that you started to draw, is that right?

Jess: Yes, so I was with Josh for just under two years and I did everything under the sun, including drawing up designs and sketching. In the evenings I had also started going to a life drawing class with my other friend, called Josh, again to keep creative and to chill out. I put some of my drawings from the class on Instagram and people started getting interested in buying them but I had no idea how to go about selling them. It was actually my mum that came up with the name Tits and Toes as those were the areas I was best at drawing.

Lynne: Ha! That's amazing.

Jess: If I had a back to draw then I'd be like, 'Oh I hate drawing backs!' I never drew a full figure and I also focused on close-ups. Then my friend Josh wrote the name Tits and Toes down and put it on a business card for my birthday, and that became my logo. I started looking into printing the drawings and it all developed from there.

Lynne: So then you went from working for Joshua to Patrick (Grant, owner of E.Tautz).

Jess: I left Josh in January 2017 and went off to New Zealand, which was really nice and definitely what I needed. When I came back I wasn't really sure what I was doing so I returned to London. I was doing some drawing, but I also needed a job, so I messaged Patrick and asked if he needed any help with his show. He offered me a position in his shop so I went and worked there full-time and continued to draw on the side – and I've actually just gone down to part-time so I can concentrate on drawing and get more done.

Lynne: I think the thing that really worked for you was when you doodled on the window of E.Tautz, then all of a sudden things started happening.

Jess: I helped with the fashion show for E.Tautz and did some backstage drawing – not live but of the images that were taken that day and Patrick saw them and said, 'Oh you should get them put up in the shop', so we did and they went on sale and I sold three out of four of them.

Lynne: *squeals with delight* Wow, that's huge!

Jess: I was like, 'oh wow, that's amazing' – I hadn't expected that sort of response at all. So then I did the drawing on the window – which was really interesting and something I'd never done before. After that, Fox Brothers got in touch as they'd seen it and they commissioned me to do some drawings of their spring/summer collection. So I did five and then they commissioned me to do another five.

Lynne: That takes us up to now: you are working part-time with Patrick and are going full steam ahead with Tits and Toes, plus you're also doing fashion commissions?

Jess: That's right. So, during fashion week, I got emailed by Delpozo – they wanted to commission me to live-draw backstage at their show. I'd never done that before, which was scary. It was so busy – all the models are moving around all over the place and I didn't feel like I had the authority to ask them to hold still for a second. There were also lots of photographers, film crews and make-up artists, plus hairdressers, around too. And there I was with my pastels and sketch book trying to get it all as fast as I could! But it went really well and I was asked to do some more – including one of an actual catwalk which meant I had to draw much faster. But I went away and developed them overnight. That was in February 2018.

Lynne: It has just snowballed for you. But you've worked your butt off. What are you wanting to do in the long run? Draw full-time?

Jess: Ideally, yes. I've got enough space to work from home but I don't know if I could do it full-time because, if I did, I'd need a studio to make sure I had a social element to my working day. Working from home seven days a week would be too anti-social. I need to get out and meet people, and the shop allows me to do that. If I was working from home all the time I'd just become a hermit. But I do want to draw during Fashion Week, collaborate with more brands and do more live drawing.

Lynne: The live drawings sounds so exciting – we live in an age where we see a million pictures being taken by people so there is something really beautiful about slowing down the process of recording shows.

Jess: Yeah, I feel like fashion illustration is definitely coming back. Quite a few of the brands have had live illustrators backstage and I think they like a different angle to show to their customers: a more authentic creative view.

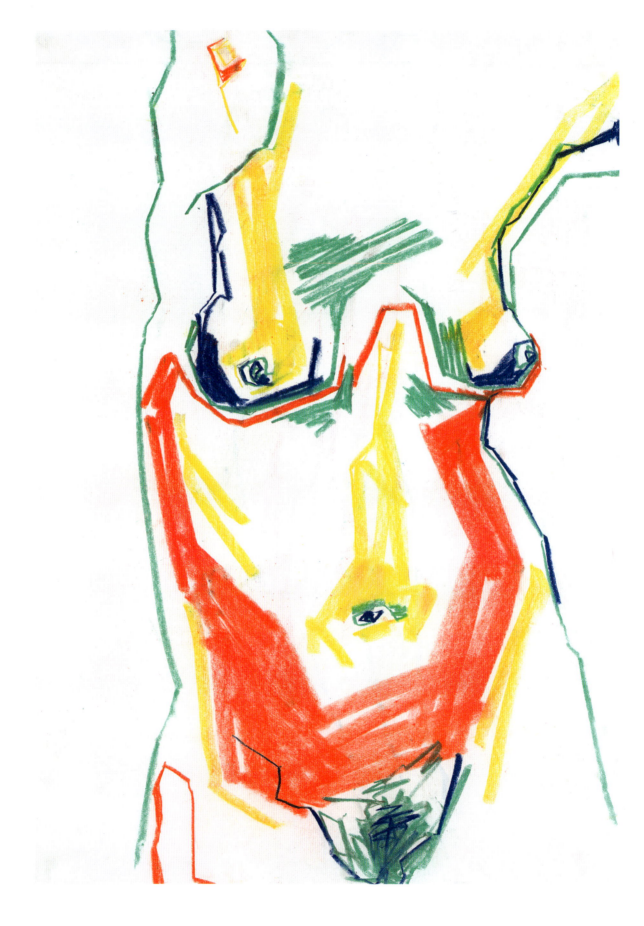

Mathematics of the Face

Is beauty in the eye of the beholder
or is it just another algorithm?

Images by Aleksandra Modrzejewska

The Golden Ratio

noun a mathematical ratio that, when achieved,
conveys the ultimate aesthetically pleasing result.

STOP.

Change.

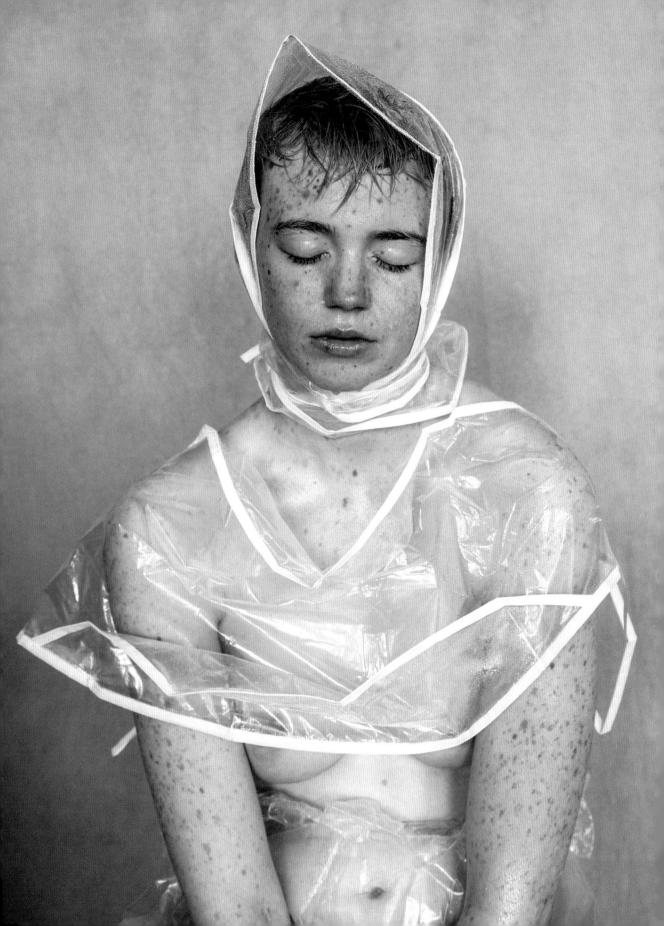

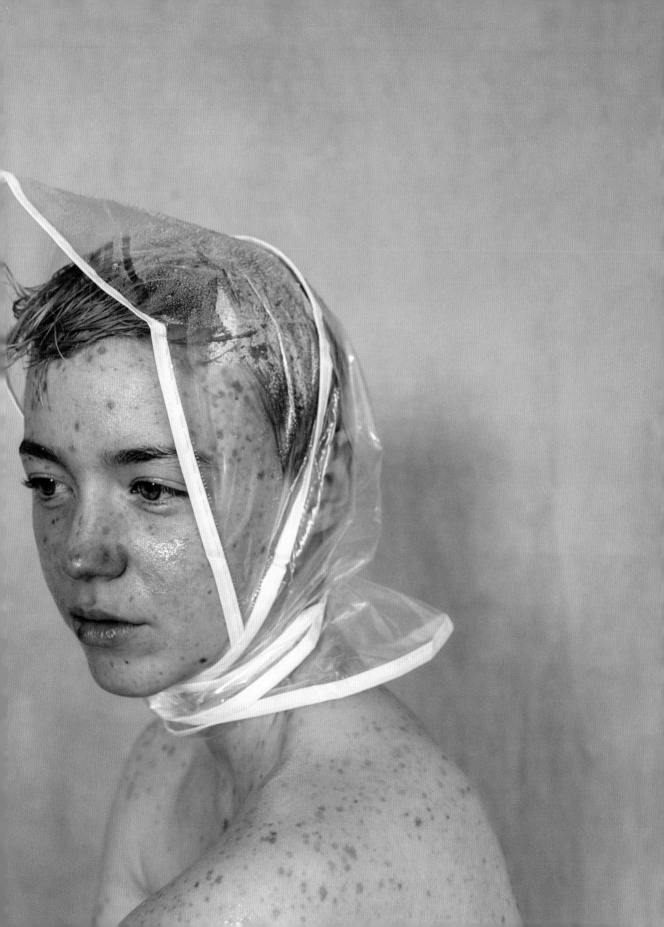

Think.

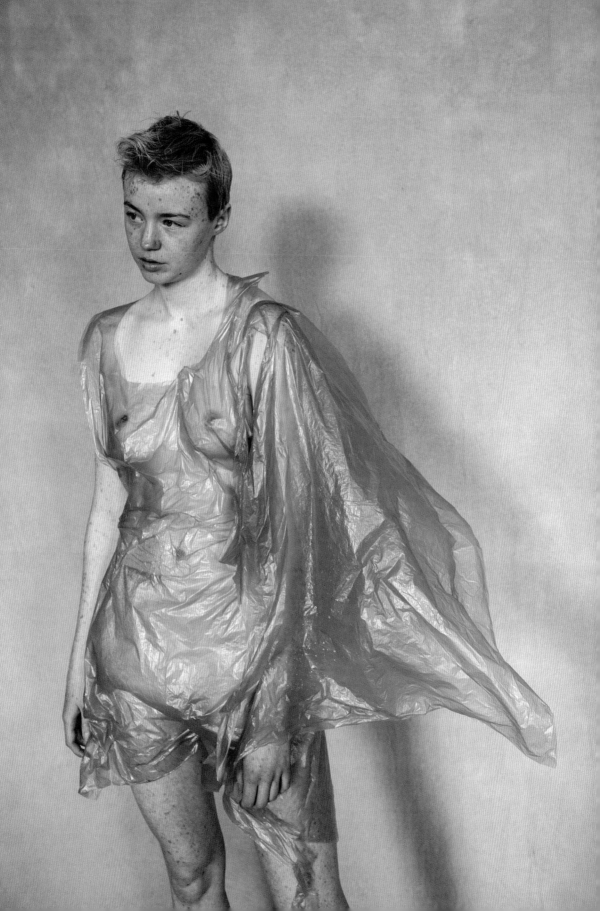

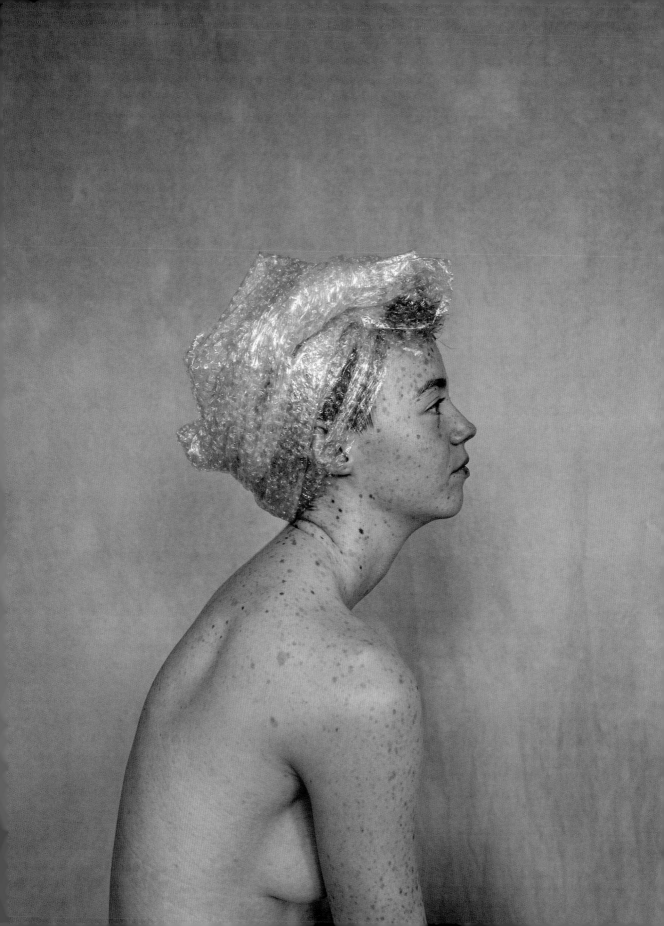

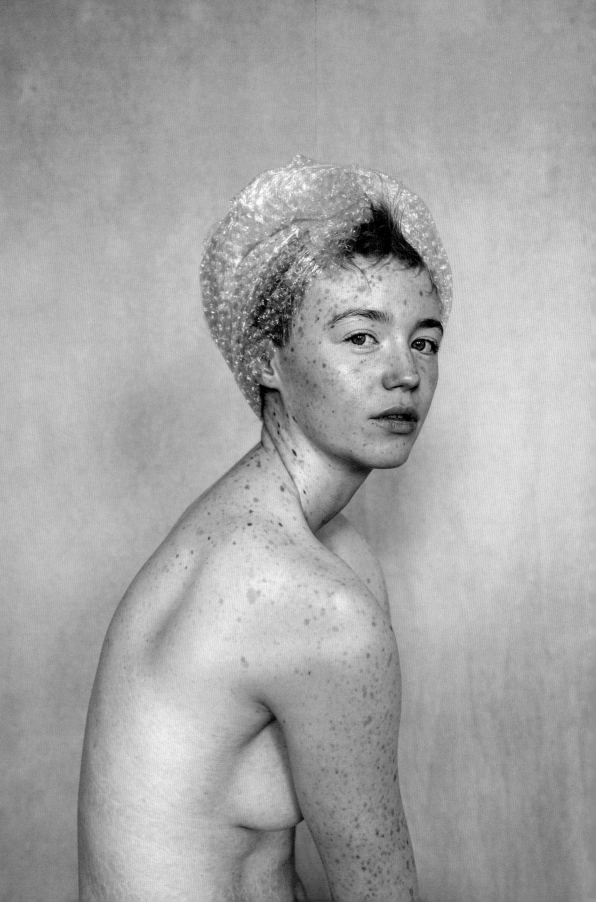

One Thousand Years.

One Bottle.

You *are* eating *it* too

On a cluttered table-top in the bathroom, I count forty-seven pieces of plastic.

The plastic contains my hair products, from washing to styling. Encases cleansers, toners and serums from a plethora of brands.

It carries soap, toothpaste, dental floss, disposable razors, baby wipes, nappy cream, teething rings, those bags we're forced to use at the airport for our liquids now.

It is moulded into unnaturally yellow rubber ducks, a redundant baby bath, multicoloured cups with holes in them to stimulate little minds while they perform their nightly ablutions. Fake fish with robotic tails, feather-light balls that float on the surface of the water while the kids splash. A bubble machine in the shape of a whale.

And right there the memory returns like a freight train to the soul.

While safely nursing my newborn on our couch I weep silently in solidarity for the mother pilot whale unable to let go of her dead calf who had been poisoned by ingesting plastic pollution in our seas.

The institution that is Sir David Attenborough narrates the footage with a heavy heart and, as the nation switches off his latest episode of *Blue Planet*, we dust off our stiff-upper-lip and go about our business making mental notes to implement changes into our day-to-day lives.

But plastic is everywhere, and we are programmed not to see it. The stuff surrounds us, suffocating the seas for our convenience. Slipping into our food chain due to our slovenly ways.

So maybe it is karmic justice for our infringement upon sealife that we ingest up to 11,000 tiny pieces of plastic annually while chowing down on that freshly battered fish with chips…

Plastic

We're
programmed
not to
see it

Images & art direction by Aleksandra Modrzejewska

Styling & concept by Lynne Coleman

Model: Georgia Valenti

the more acceptable it is as the status quo.

In the summer, these contrasts always feel more intense. In winter there are a few places that open up for the homeless, but in the heat of the summer the trash on the street steams and the homeless people sit alongside it. It is a side to the city you rarely see on screen – there is this sticky sense of oppression. The excess of this rotting food on the street contrasts horribly with those who have no food. It's intense.

Some restaurants will give their leftovers to the homeless, but not many can because there are so many rules and regulations that would prevent it. It's a city with so much red tape. No one wants to get sued. So you end up protecting yourself ahead of helping others.

It is a city that pulls extremes, and it's hard not to be extreme in it.

In the UK, the Deliveroo concept is still relatively new but, in New York, it's already well established. You can have salad, Thai food, soup, Middle Eastern food, fried chicken, literally any kind of food you like delivered directly to your door, 24/7, but the poverty of the city is in your face at the same time. As you walk around, this poverty is a reminder that everyone is just one pay check away from potentially being out on the street.

That's the kind of city you live in when you live in New York: there is no safety net. The healthcare system is really screwed and you can be sacked from a job without a notice period.

We covered a story at one stage with a woman who was working as a nurse. She broke her leg and her health care covered her only so far, but not far enough. Her leg hadn't really healed so she wasn't able to work, this led to her losing her job and within two months she was on the street. She was a professional woman with a skill. She was fortunate enough that there was a great business at the time that cared for people on the street so she was able to get back on her feet and find another job with their help, but that was really rare. It's fascinating: situations like these are tragic and horrendous when you first arrive in the city but the longer you live in there,

My bestie and editor of New York based magazine, W42st, *and I discuss dinner and disillusionment in the city that never sleeps, in a world of extremes where people have plenty or nothing.*

New York is a city of extremes like no other: the temperature is icy cold in the winter and super steamy in the summer; iconic old buildings, like the Chrysler Building and the Empire State Building, contrast with glass and steel pencil structures that just shoot up into the sky; and vast wealth exists alongside appalling poverty. Because Manhattan is all on an island, the only place to go is up. Everything is contained in a small area where wealthy stockbrokers are cheek by jowl with homeless people, and one of the hardest things to come to terms with is that these contrasts don't seem weird after you have lived there for a while.

So I think the concept of being able to access copious amounts of food – any ethnicity of cuisine, regardless of whether it is day or night – whilst being around such appalling hunger and poverty is harrowing.

It is hard not to be extreme in New York. Once you get there you ask yourself: 'What are people running from?' They are out every night as if they're afraid of missing something, but it is difficult not to be out and even harder not to get dragged into a mentality that there must alwaysbe something happening. So to actually say no, and take back some balance, requires discipline.

We've All Got To Eat

In conversation with Ruth Walker

Images by Nick Policarpo

Make-up and art direction by Molly Jane Sheridan

Models: Belle Sansone, Jason Witcher and Sucia

Thanks to Gotham West Market

I try and think about what her needs are, or how she wants to walk into a room or drop her kids off at school, what she needs at each part of her day. You know, I see that the world has become super casual and actually much more relaxed towards how we dress. When we think about work wear, for example, it has become a lot less formal. On the other hand, there is event dressing, for when you really want to switch it up to party. So there are still extremes. A lot of people are very casual and trainers have become a staple in daywear, people want that kind of comfort. Our lives are much easier and not as groomed. For example, wearing a dress for lunch – that kind of dressing up just doesn't seem as relevant or in tune with our lives anymore.

Lynne: Yes, it's no longer how we live. Everything has become more relaxed for 'statement dressing' which is documented on social media. So what about you, how does your online/offline life filter into the brand?

Osman: I can't really believe I am a millennial. I mean, from a personal point of view, I missed the whole Facebook generation because I'm quite a private person fundamentally and I don't want to be sharing my whole life with everyone around the world. But I do have to actually engage with social media to tell our story and convey the ethos of what we are trying to do as a brand. That's where you need to have communication with your customer: giving them insight and creating a community online, and I have to offer myself as part of that conversation. It is a difficult for me – but I try to let go; you know, it is what it is.

Lynne: Yes, I think everyone is actually a little scared of it right now, but what you are communicating is your work and that's the part people are connecting to.

Osman: Yeah, I'm not the 'hey look at me' kind of a person – I'd rather be empowering women and make them feel fabulous through my designs. I always want to take a back seat behind women.

Sarah Murray (pictured) is the owner of the award-winning boutique, Jane Davidson, and advisor at atterley.com. She has been wearing and stocking Osman for five years.

Lynne: So what is the first step in these nine-month cycles, what happens at the beginning?

Osman: The design process happens first. So right now I'm working on a project due in September, which will be done in August. I'll also start working in July on the pre-fall range, which delivers in November. So you basically have to simultaneously develop four collections at the same time.

Lynne: That's intense.

Osman: Yeah, it is really intense. The collections are all layered on top of each other. But that's the whole idea around range plans and best sellers: you can keep on selling throughout the year.

Lynne: Do you feel like there are some key elements in the process of designing clothes that you always refer back to?

Osman: We are trying to do something called 'the perfect five' which is our modular wardrobe. We are trying to make those pieces as sustainable as possible. By sustainable we mean the items have low mileage, are produced locally so the fabric hasn't been flown from halfway across the world to be manufactured in one place and then flown back again; and are made from some form of organic, recyclable yarn. We want each of the pieces in 'the perfect five' to touch one of these points, if not two, with everything trying to touch three. I know there's a couple of pieces which do touch three, but at least everything is touching one marker of what sustainability is for us.

Lynne: What prompted this?

Osman: You know, I just feel like we all have to make an effort to reduce our global footprint. If you are complaining about the kind of food you want to eat and what goes inside your body then what you wear is important as well.

Lynne: So where do you get the head space to be creative whilst juggling up to three collections at one time?

Osman: Well, you just have to find the head space. The pre-collections have to be more formulaic and range plan oriented, but with the main collections you have room to be more creative with the message that you want to put out onto the runway.

Lynne: And who is your muse? Who's your girl? Is there someone in your head that you design for? What kind of fictional character is she?

Osman: She is a range of people. She's from her mid-twenties up to her fifties.

Osman: Sorry I missed your call earlier, I was out getting a drink when you rang. But guess where I am now? I'm in a little park around the corner and it has some swings so I feel like I've gone back to my childhood.

Lynne: Oh how lovely! Well, my one-year-old is sleeping upstairs so we have kids everywhere today!

Osman: These are the most uncomfortable swings, they look like nappies...

Lynne: Are you sitting on one of them?

Osman: Yeah!

laughter.

Seconds later some plonker asks Osman to move off said swing in an empty park since he isn't a child. We chuckle, surely swings are for everyone?

* * *

Lynne: So, there's the business side of what you do, then there's the design side but it's all very circular – right?

Osman: Yeah, it's seasonal and it doesn't stop.

Lynne: It never stops, and I think people get sucked into this romantic idea that every season, and year, is different when, actually, you are churning out fashion formulas.

Osman: Yes, there are four deliveries a year. There is constant pressure to provide new products all the time.

Lynne: And you've been doing this now for how long?

Osman: Ten years.

Lynne: Have you seen that the industry has become more ferocious over the decade?

Osman: Definitely. You know, we are a smaller brand and we've grown really organically so we're in a good place. But the business side is hard, because the cash flow cycle is crazy. You spend your money, start developing a collection for three months then it goes into a show, then there's the sales campaign for a month, then you need another three months to produce it. So really the whole process of creating, showcasing and selling the products is all done in nine months – then, when you deliver it, people want you to give ninety-day terms. So the money you spend in month one you don't get back until month nine.

Lynne: And of course everyone along the way needs paid. The team, models, factories...

Osman: Absolutely.

In Conversation with Osman

Images by Ellie Morag

Make-up by Jen Beattie at Violet Rose make-up artistry

Model: Sarah Murray

Styling and concept by Lynne Coleman

end up feeling like you're missing out and end up comparing yourself to your peers. You just need to remind yourself we're all on the journey we're supposed to go on and someone else's success doesn't take away from your own,' Amanda adds.

Yet, for all its sins the algorithm is here to stay. And that means not gaming but instead continuing to create, connect and do work that you are proud of.

Colour and quirk may not be the route for growth but for Amanda it's a case of questioning – 'How do you appeal to the mass market when you don't want to?' Simply put, you don't.

It's not so much about quick growth and stacking up those numbers, it's finding your niche – whether that's your personality, photography, beauty or style, and building on it over time. The algorithm has taught us that we need an instant hit, and, while it can be a stepping stone, it's not the only way up.

Social media has made it easier than ever to find the weird and wonderful, the people who spark fire in your soul. While the algorithm may make that ultimately more difficult, there's beauty in the binary.

We've forgotten what people look like in between the face tunes and filters. Social media can be an amazing place of discovery and creativity, like a digital mood board of things that inspire you – but more often than not it's seen as a way of saying who you are and presenting a defined sense of self. It's a highlight reel, with all the best bits cherry picked for your consideration. It's not real. It doesn't have to be either. But when style and beauty feel homogenised it can all begin to feel a little bit soulless.

'If the algorithm had its way it would all be "jeans and nice top". People do follow people for their looks. I remember seeing a poll on whether people followed people for looks and style. Forty-five per cent said looks and I wasn't surprised. You see young girls getting Botox and fillers. In the same breath though, Instagram has allowed me to be more accepting of my body and be kinder. It's complicated,' Sheri adds.

All of this can have an impact. It took me a while to realise the follower count didn't directly correlate to my talent or skillset (and ultimately self-worth.) I drove myself sick with jealousy, insecurity and a whole host of bad feelings over numbers. It's a love/hate relationship and I'd be lying if I didn't second (third, fourth) guess everything I put on my feed. The algorithm more often than not can be that little voice that feeds your anxiety, reminding you that you're not good enough.

For Sheri the algorithm is an added weight. 'I struggle to see the positive side [of the algorithm] as I feel like it stifles creativity. The best way I would describe my anxiety is like a fat man sitting on my chest, and when I post something I love and it doesn't do well, the fat guy gains a few pounds. What I have to remember is that my posts are based on a computer programme and that isn't a measure of my skill or worth. I just need to keep on creating.'

'It's something I can't control and that itself stressed me out. When you create something you love and it isn't popular it's hard not to take it personally. It makes you doubt yourself and, yeah, has made me cry on a few occasions. It's hard not to let the green eyed monster come out to play – and sometimes living in Scotland you

The algorthim itself may challenge creativity but it's hard to argue against its popularisation of a certain kind of beauty standard. The Instagram face is alive and well, and certain 'it' items read like a shopping list of things that will generate more likes.

While social media has allowed for niche communities to grow and flourish, the algorithm instead plays to a homogenisation of style. A click through the explore page can be a testament to that.

'I've never been cool and the algorithm can make it feel like you're at high school. You're competing with this socially accepted face. This shouldn't be what people aspire to look like. We should be striving to be the best version of ourselves and believe that we are good enough. I never want to dress for likes and, while I know my style is naturally evolving, I also make sure it's natural and not coming from some external pressure to conform. I follow people who push their own aesthetic boundaries. They may not be at the top of the explore page but they are who inspire me,' Amanda explains.

'Instagram stories allow you to be more accessible and try new things. There's a difference between monitoring and letting the algorithm dictate what you post. I'm a visual person and love the idea of snapshots of people's lives, and to a degree some of that feels lost. The algorithm has raised the stakes in every sense of the word. I've carved my slice of the internet based on authenticity rather than aspiration. I want to give people a piece of me and not just my content. If I went on what was successful my feed would be entirely selfies and that wouldn't satisfy me creatively. I do things I enjoy – and the algorithm challenges that.'

Amanda doesn't see how the algorithm can encourage creativity and thinks it is more of a chokehold. 'It's all thought out and it's not as enjoyable. It's become more to do with popularity than fun. I've got to be tactical. As a fashion blogger, I love talking about clothes and designers so it's disheartening when my most engaged pictures are of my face. I want to push my fashion content and the things I love but it's figuring out how. Is it street style, is it being more avant garde – you are constantly learning and it's constantly changing.'

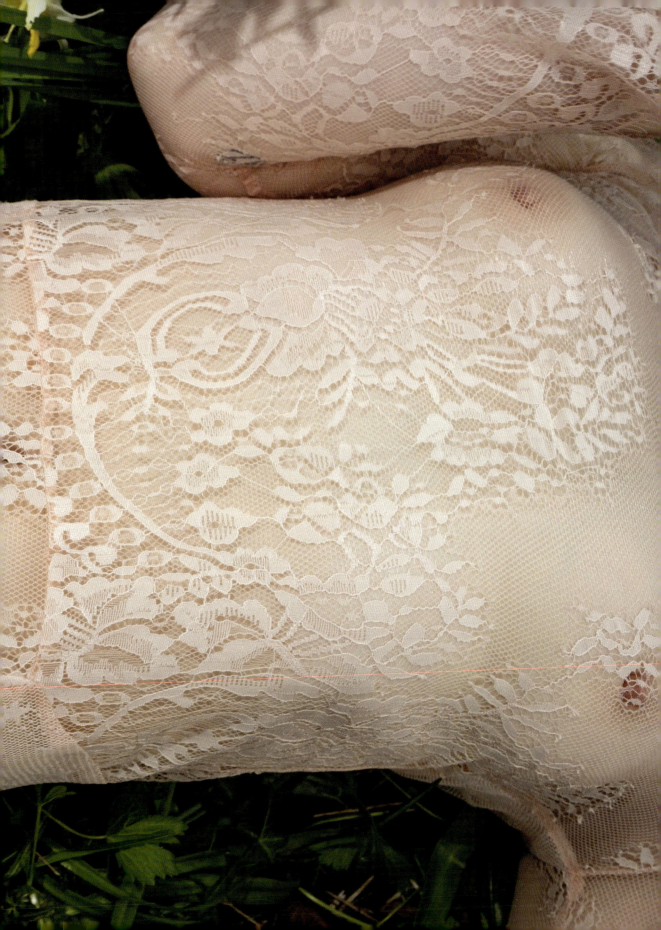

Social media, for better or for worse, has become a bit of a numbers game. While there seems to be a near constant plea for the return of the chronological timeline (pretty please?), the algorithm is here to stay. Which means thinking tactically, posting strategically and, even with all of that, hoping for the best. For better or for worse, social media is how I find work and, for my friends, it makes up part of their office. The algorithm has gone from being a pesky piece of code to metamorphosing into the monster under every blogger's bed. From holding creativity hostage to fostering self doubt, who's afraid of the big bad algorithm?

Well it turns out, when your livelihood depends on it, quite a lot of people. For Amanda, the personal and private are so intermingled that it is difficult to separate the social digital and the social 'real life':

'It's no longer a snapshot of your life, it's curated content posted to a time schedule. It takes away from the instant platform that it used to be. From small companies to micro-influencers, the algorithm affects us personally and financially due to the push for monetisation. You're constantly aware of it.'

For Sheri, the algorithm takes away a little bit of the creative part of the soul. 'The thing about the algorithm is that it removes the emotion, asking you to play in to a system designed for more clicks. There's no heartbeat.'

Creativity to a degree has become commercialised – you're no longer posting just for the scroll but for the feed. When you receive your next pay cheque can depend on your engagement, it can be difficult to take risks and can take away from the joy of creating. On one hand, it can be a way to push you to be better, creating a more well-thought out approach to posting – but it can also take away an element of play and experimentation.

'You want to showcase your work but at times it feels like your creativity is held to ransom. I post less now and have become more self-critical. I want to make something I'm proud of but before I would create more often. It can be frustrating when you put in a lot of time and energy yet receive no reward. The excitement is gone,' Sheri tells me.

Colour Cult

How three women talk to
100,000 followers
Foreveryoursbetty,
Honeypopkisses & Beewaits chat
Algorithms & Anxiety

Images by Brian Sweeney
Concept and styling by Lynne Coleman
Words by Claire Stuart

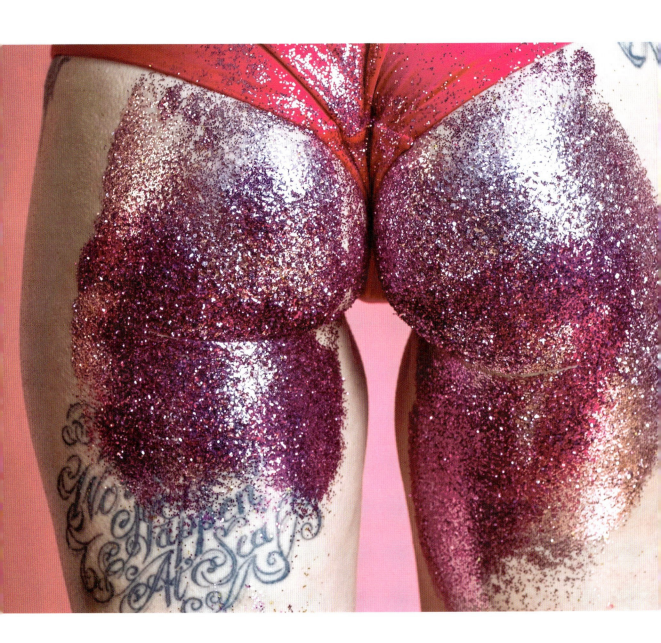

relationship. However, it is not lost on me that millions of women, past, present and future, have been or will be in similar situations without successful exits.

Had I been born one hundred years before in the same set of circumstances, would I have been institutionalised or medicated for wanting to leave a marriage with my then three-year-old?

If Zelda Fitzgerald and I swapped lives, would she have thrived and fulfilled her own creative journey?

This year has been a lightning rod to the roles we play in society. It's too simplistic to say that the divide is gender specific. Each of us, irrespective of chromosomes, have schizophrenic personas at different points of the day. We are friends, siblings, colleagues, parents, lovers, enemies, peacemakers, anarchists, activists and more. These are all contained inside our fleshy exterior, the crazy waiting to bubble up and spill over at a second's notice.

It's that natural ebb and flow of life that can lead us into dark places as a society. If I had a tear for every time I read a judgmental statement this past year – be it on #metoo or repealing the 8th amendment – I'd have cried a river. Luckily, the antidote to the bile came from empathetic thinkers realising that, if we don't speak up, bigotry bellows.

But, regardless of the volume generated by people who hate, we all have the opportunity not to be repressed, to stand up and tell our story rather than accept that of the person shouting the loudest.

When you do finally look in the mirror the reflection bears little resemblance to what went before. Motherhood is a metamorphosis. Clinging onto the previous body, thought processes and lifestyle would be as preposterous as the caterpillar craving life as larva now it's a butterfly.

In a happy place, this transition is smooth like chocolate melting on the tongue. In a not-so-happy place it's like chomping into an unripened strawberry. It looks good on the outside but bitter to bite and difficult to swallow. However, you get on with it, for fear of judgement should you spit it out.

Self-censorship leads to the kind of repression that comes back later in life like a wrecking ball.

Failing to say when we are unhappy for fear of hurting people inevitably leads to everyone becoming unhappy and hurt. But, as women, we have learned to silence ourselves in exchange for our safety – it happens so subtly we barely recognise the behavioural change.

I am guilty of such behaviour. In trying to get out of a situation I no longer wanted to be part of, I acted irrationally and recklessly. I didn't feel strong enough to leave. I had been programmed for over a decade into believing that I was incapable of doing anything on my own, that I wasn't quite good enough and that I had never achieved anything other than failure. Powerful messages when delivered by a person you perceive as a loved one.

By the time I managed to unglue myself from that person's opinion, things got nasty. I was told I had mental health problems as that was the only plausible reason for wanting to leave. This message was relayed to my mother, in-laws, best friends and neighbours at an alarming rate. I was urged into counselling to see the error of my ways, being told I would soon see how my mental health was affecting my ability to see clearly. It transpired to be the exact lifeline I needed to leave, the clarity from an external third party alerting me to the dangers of staying in such a

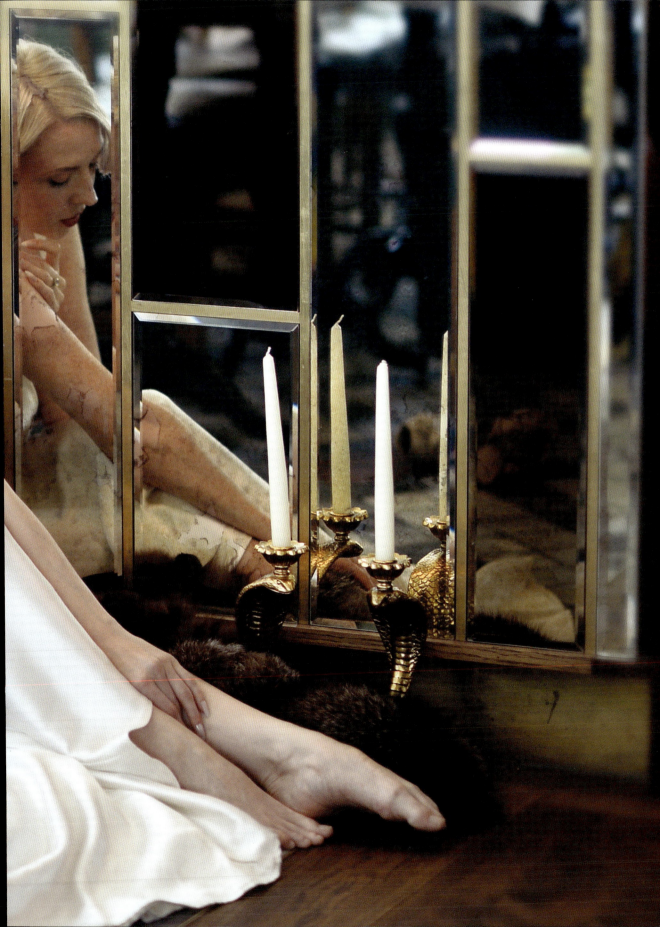

In the fog of nesting, neurones misfire from underuse. It's not like before, the warmth of our home feels like the Disney-definition of family.

Mon coeur is cocooned in diabetic-coma-inducing levels of sugary love.

You see this is not my first rodeo, baby number two from marriage part deux amplifies the past like a flood lit echo chamber. Recall reverberates around the room until all flashbacks are lulled into submission. This is on the understanding that muscle memory doesn't have to mean making the same mistakes twice.

As you slowly emerge from the other side of baby slumber, wading through that heavy hanging post-natal fog can be tiresome. It has been such a long time since you've felt like yourself that you can miss the signals of spring postpartum.

Ode To Zelda

Images by Julie Howden

Concept by Lynne Coleman

Make-up by Jen Beattie at Violet Rose make-up artistry

Thanks to The Ivy on the Square

'Plagiarism begins at home'
Zelda Fitzgerald, 1922
New York Tribune

ALEKSANDRA MODRZEJEWSKA – PHOTOGRAPHER

For years I have stalked this girl online. We have the same friends, work with the same people and live in the same city, but our paths have never crossed until this book. I tentatively reached out to Aleksandra via Instagram – I have such a girl crush on her and am a massive fan of her work so I waited with baited breath to hear her reply. Luckily for me, she is as gracious and kind as she is talented. Creating 'Plastic' with her felt like second nature, despite it being our first shoot together. She is an artist in the truest sense.

CLAIRE STUART – WRITER

There are many things I could write about Claire. She has an incredible command of the English language, her quick-witted humour is intoxicating and she is someone you gravitate towards in a crowded room. But, above all of that, she is a loyal friend who will love you fiercely.

NUALA SWAN – PHOTOGRAPHER

It was the summer of 2014 when this ludicrously talented photographer entered my orbit. We were shooting a Harris Tweed installation at the Swedish Institute for the Edinburgh International Fashion Festival. Our model was draped over the miniature room sculpture like a giant Alice in Wonderland and Nuala shot it on analogue, forever making me love this long lost art-form.

FAL CARBERRY – OWNER OF BLOW COLOUR BAR

Fal is the most courageous and incredible boss bitch you could ever have the pleasure of meeting and the powerhouse behind the cult hair institution that is BLOW. If I had an ounce of this lady's talent I could take over the world. She is colourful and exciting and her creativity is contagious. A true hair legend in the industry already and she hasn't even started!

KATIE DANGER – STYLIST

This elegant elfin creature and I went to university together at the dawn of the new millennium. A ludicrously chic lass even as a student, I always remember watching her thinking she had the best style. Almost two decades later we've swapped the lecture halls for nursery rooms as we entertain our tiny tribes together.

the first time we met...

CHRISTINA KERNOHAN – PHOTOGRAPHER

Late 2014, Christina and I ran around a half empty brutalist building with a very young model (who happens to be on the front cover of this very book) shooting crazy couture with crazier wigs. It took us four years to get back together to create 'Emancipation'. She was pregnant with her first child while shooting this concept, which has meant so much to all of us.

ELLIE MORAG – PHOTOGRAPHER

This beautiful human came into my orbit via a mutual friend, but I had rather creepily been admiring her long before that via Instagram. Ellie's street-style studies have captured this zeitgeist explosion we find ourselves in where everyone seems to hit the pavements to picture themselves. In 2017 when I was fat, uncomfortable and pregnant we all went to London to showcase Cross Cashmere at The Groucho. The night before, she had slept on the couch in the apartment I rented, that's when I knew she was the kind of woman who was right up my street.

JEN BEATTIE – MAKE-UP ARTIST

My formative memory of the queen-of-skin-sheen is from summer 2017. I was at Hutchesons, about to speak at an event with Very Exclusive, and she wafted in with the most beautiful bouncy blow dry and skin that would make the Chrysler building look dull. After initially biting back feelings of inadequacy standing next to the full-time lawyer and mum of three who runs her own make-up artistry empire you rapidly realise something: Is she a superhero? No! She is something even better: a woman who will happily teach you how to get the glow by sharing all her hints and tips. Legend!

contributors –

BRIAN SWEENEY – PHOTOGRAPHER

We have been shooting together just shy of a decade. I first met him in a vegan bar in the earthier side of Glasgow's merchant city despite both of us being meat-eating non-hipsters. His illustrious career has seen him shoot the coolest names in entertainment for even cooler publications – but this guy is salt-of-the-earth unpretentious perfection. And no one gets my creepy warped thoughts better than he does.

MOLLY-JANE SHERIDAN – MAKE-UP ARTIST

For four years I have watched this lady blossom into one of the country's leading make-up creatives and art directors. For our first shoot together, I wanted her to turn four female olympic-medal winning athletes into their subconscious as they prepared to go for gold. She asked me to send her pictures of the kind of make-up I envisaged, I sent her images of lions with giant manes and gold coins that had faces on them. She clarified that she meant make-up looks, I told her to create her own. What she did on that warm mid-May day still sends shivers down my spine.

JULIE HOWDEN – PHOTOGRAPHER

It was 2016 when Julie and I finally got behind the lens together after working around each other for almost ten years with the same creative teams but never finding ourselves together. She was on *The Herald* side of the country, I was on *The Scotsman*, but you can't keep two gal's with the same passion apart for long. She has a great eye for theatre and opulence and I am mad for a decadent dame like that.

Contents

Contributors   2–5
Ode to Zelda   6–19
Colour Cult   20–45
In Conversation with Osman   46–63
We've All Got To Eat   64–79
Plastic   80–101

Mathematics of the Face   74–89
Tits & Toes   58–73
The Emancipation of Motherhood   40–57
Theatre of Lies   30–39
Fear   12–29
The Definition of Algorithm   6–11

Contents